This Book belongs to

Clemmie

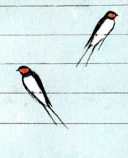

TO MY YOUNGEST SON

SINGING RASCALS DO
Original Finnish title LAULUVIIKARIN DO

This series of books is based on the teaching method developed by Géza Szilvay and is part of the instructional material used by the Colourstrings Music Kindergartens.

The melodies in the SINGING RASCALS series reappear in the colourstrings/colourkeys instrumental beginners books. Pupils find this very helpful during the early stages of learning an instrument.

For further details of Colourstrings Music Kindergartens write to the publishers:

COLOURSTRINGS INTERNATIONAL LIMITED
4 ULLSWATER CLOSE
KINGSTON VALE
LONDON SW15 3RF

Copyright © 1987 Géza Szilvay & Tuulia Hyrske & Kustannusosakeyhtiö Tammi publishers

Text: Copyright © 1991 Angela Ailes

Printed by Breckland Print Ltd, Attleborough, Norfolk, England.

ISBN 1 873604 02 5

SINGING RASCALS
DO

Géza Szilvay

Illustrations:
Tuulia Hyrske

Words:
Angela Ailes

SONGS:

DASHING DAN	4
MY DOLLY MOLLY	6
LITTLE TRAIN	8
ELSIE THE ELEPHANT	10
COWBOY JOE	12
MOUSEY	14
CHUCK CHUCK CHICKENS	16
INCY WINCY SPIDER	18

COLOURSTRINGS INTERNATIONAL LIMITED
LONDON

DASHING DAN

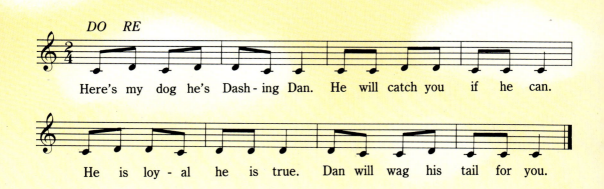

MY DOLLY MOLLY

MI
RE
DO

LITTLE TRAIN

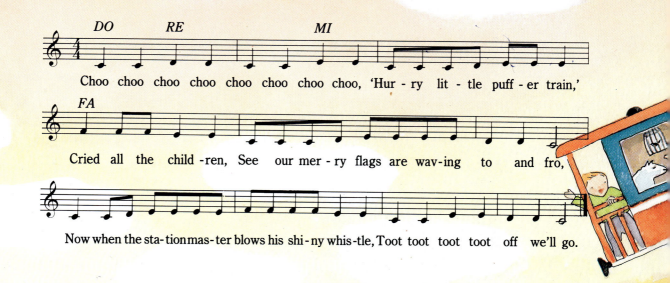

FA
MI
MI
RE
DO

ELSIE THE ELEPHANT

DO   *RE MI*

El - sie is an el - e - phant who wants to play. She is

SO

mus - ic - al and big and grey. She is good at sing - ing Mi Re

FA

Do. That's why the lit - tle child - ren love her so.

COWBOY JOE

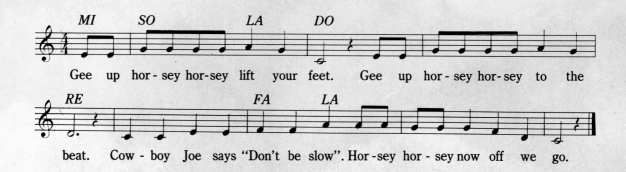

MOUSEY

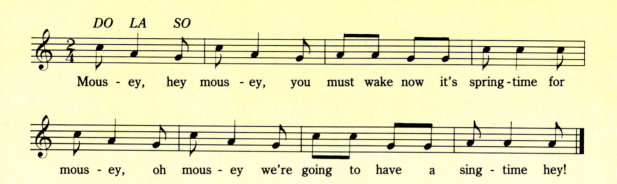

DO
LA
SO

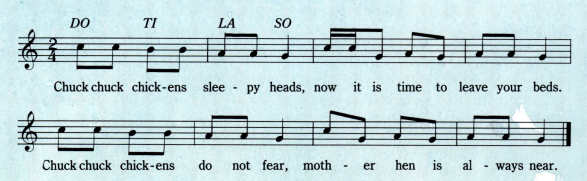

INCY WINCY SPIDER

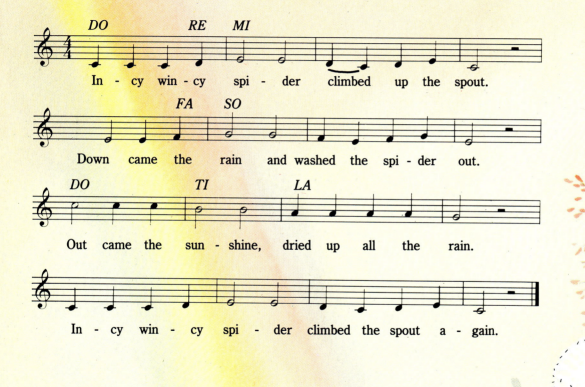

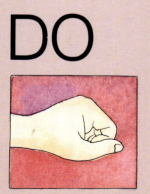

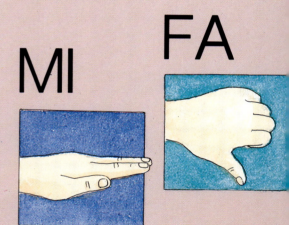

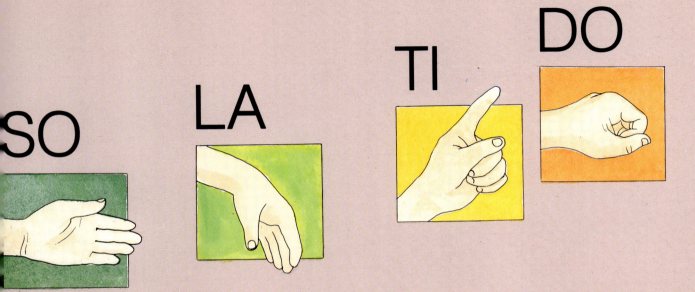

MESSAGE FROM DR. GÉZA SZILVAY
Head of the East Helsinki Music Institute and compiler of the "Singing Rascals" series

Many children today have all the material things they need: clothes, food, toys, etc; sometimes they have more than enough. Material things, however, cannot replace the warmth affection and time we give to the child, which is so important for its spiritual nourishment.

The "Singing Rascals" books are intended as a means of helping parents, grandparents, kindergarten and nursery school teachers, and all those who have children in their care, to create stimulating and purposeful moments with them.

The pictures, melodies, and words in these books have been carefully chosen and arranged with young pre-school children in mind. The tunes have been selected from those which over the years have proved appealing and easy to learn, and are skilfully illustrated. The characters may be used to make up tales arising from the songs. The printed notation is only for the use of the adults.

The songs progress from two notes up to five notes (pentatonic) or seven notes (diatonic). Although for the sake of clarity they are written in C major and A minor, singing them in different keys, i.e. from different starting notes, is to be encouraged, thus suiting the children's own pitch registers. The use of solfa marking (Do-Re) makes it easy for parents to learn basic solmisation while the children enjoy learning the pitch names and hand signs.

The series is supported by a parallel series of audio tapes on which infants sing and young children perform the melodies, but no cassette, however good, can replace the lap and guidance of the close relative or friend.

The creation of Colourstrings Music Kindergartens is a significant step forward in the music education of the very young, and one in which I feel proud to play a part. My wish for all the little members is – joyous singing!

Géza Szilvay

Composers:

Dashing Dan
Jorma Ollaranta.

My Dolly Molly
*

The Little Train
*

Elsie the Elephant
*

Cowboy Joe
*

Mousey
Zoltán Kodály
© 1962 by Zoltán Kodály
Copyright assigned 1964 to
Boosey & Hawkes Music Publishers Ltd
Revised edition copyright 1970 by
Boosey & Hawkes Music Publishers Ltd
Reprinted by permission of
Boosey & Hawkes Music Publishers Ltd

Chuck Chuck Chickens
*

Incy Wincy Spider
*

*Tunes based on children's and folk melodies.